Christopher Columbus

A Captivating Guide to the Life of an Italian Explorer and His Voyages to the Americas

Free Bonus from Captivating History
(Available for a Limited time)

Hi History Lovers!

Now you have a chance to join our exclusive history list so you can get your first history ebook for free as well as discounts and a potential to get more history books for free! Simply visit the link below to join.

Captivatinghistory.com/ebook

Also, make sure to follow us on Facebook, Twitter and Youtube by searching for Captivating History.

Contents

Introduction

Christopher Columbus was one of the most courageous of the world's explorers. He embraced risk in an era when the blinding expanse of the Atlantic Ocean frightened the Europeans.

The cartography of the day was incorrect, as he learned through bitter experience. Columbus is credited with the discovery of America but never realized it during his lifetime. His career as a navigator was peppered with mishaps that shattered the ignorance of the age. Although he was no scientist, Columbus initiated new fields of study and analysis.

In 1492, he landed at San Salvador in the Islands of the Bahamas, and he was the first European to have explored the Caribbean Sea. He was the first European to set foot in Cuba, Haiti, and Trinidad, as well as the countries in Central America. Columbus's voyages astonished all of Europe and started a virtual stampede of competitors in search of the East Indies by sailing west.

These pages will uncover the most interesting aspects of the life of Christopher Columbus. For example, most accounts of Columbus have overlooked the fact that he was an advertiser and a salesman of extraordinary ability.

His life was fraught with adversities such as betrayal and character assassination. It still is today. However, his loyalty cannot be assailed, and few have recognized that fact.

The life of Christopher Columbus is a fascinating portrayal of a man whose ego was greater than his common sense. His brand of reckless abandon makes Olympic champions out of foolhardy amateurs. This is the story of a man devoted to a goal he was willing to pursue or die trying. And, tragically, he did die trying.

Chapter 1 – Into the Blue Unknown

As a boy, Christopher Columbus, or "Cristoforo Columbo," as it would be spelled in Italian, worked his father's loom in their shop in the port city of Genoa in Italy. Outside the window were quays and wharves. The shadows of the large sailing ships, such as three-masted caravels, blocked his light and attracted his interest. He watched in fascination as the swarthy sailors spoke strange tongues and unloaded crates of cotton from Egypt, silk from India, and raw wool from northern England—the uncleaned version of what Columbus used in his father's shop. As a young man, Christopher was fascinated by the sea. The whispers of the salty air called him, and he responded.

Importance of Trade

The ports of Italy were busy during the Renaissance years. There was much money to be made at the fairs and markets from selling gold, spices, unspun cotton, and leather goods. Many boys of the day started out helping on the ships as cabin boys and worked their way up the ranks. In 1470, twenty-year-old Columbus secured employment with René of Anjou, who was called the "king" of Naples. The wealthy families of Italy fought bitterly for control of land in Italy, and René's family, the House of Anjou, lost Naples to

Ferdinand of Aragon in Spain. René of Anjou engaged Columbus' services for about four years in a futile effort to regain Naples. Columbus had no stake in Naples; he was a pilot, the occupational name for a captain. Columbus was a man of the sea, not the land.

In 1477, he sailed to Lisbon in Portugal and met with his brother, Bartholomew. Columbus claimed that seafaring city as his hometown for several years. In Lisbon, he met Filipa, the daughter of Bartolomeu Perestrello, the governor of Porto Santo Island in the archipelago of Madeira. They married in 1479 or 1480. He and Filipa had a son, Diego.

The prince of Portugal, Henry, later known as "Prince Henry the Navigator," shared Columbus's interest in seafaring and created a college for mariners. Columbus had access to the libraries there and studied the sea charts of the times. In addition, he studied the books of the humanistic scholars, geometry, and cartography. Both Bartholomew and Christopher Columbus became very skilled in drawing maps of the sea, and it is said that both worked at this profession.

Columbus sailed the Mediterranean, which was full of pirates. He sailed to Crimea, Tunis, Greece, Sicily, Spain, and England. In 1481, Columbus piloted a fleet of ten caravels to Guinea, on Africa's northwestern coast.

He had aboard the distinguished Admiral Azumbago, whom he took to the Cape Verde Islands just off the coast of Guinea. There, the African king greeted them, and they gifted him with hawks and horses. It was customary to present gifts to the rulers of various countries and was also an effective way to prevent hostilities.

To buy the exotic goods from the Far East, traders had to take land routes by horse or camel and toil their way across Asia. These routes went through land controlled by the Mongols, who generally protected those traveling the "Silk Road" because it contributed to their economy. After the fall of the Mongolian Empire, however, the Ottoman Turks took over. The Turks weren't as obliging and failed to protect travelers as they journeyed. Therefore, many never returned.

To avoid being attacked by marauders, Europeans were desirous of finding an alternate route to China and India by crossing the Atlantic Ocean. Most educated people of the Age of Discovery had realized the Atlantic wasn't infested with sea monsters, and many considered attempting the voyage. Elements of danger still lurked there, but the objective of wealth whetted their appetites to explore.

Portugal was extremely active in establishing maritime routes, especially in the South Atlantic. For many years, they created colonies in the South Atlantic and explored the West African coast. When returns from Africa failed to meet their expectations, the Portuguese craved the riches of India. In 1488, Bartholomew Dias proved that India could be reached by sailing around Africa. However, it was an impractical and dangerous journey. The cartographers of the time hadn't predicted the existence of another continent, so they envisioned an Atlantic voyage as a logical possibility.

Columbus was living and working for merchants in Portugal when discussions about the viability of a voyage west to the Indies was the topic of the day. Columbus, a man of humble origin, seized the opportunity to reach beyond his social status and gain wealth and fame. However, Christopher Columbus was also a man filled with limitless curiosity. He asked questions and was dissatisfied until he found the answers.

So, he and his brother, Bartholomew, decided to approach the king and queen of Portugal to finance a voyage.

The Portuguese Proposal

Columbus was an excellent marketer who never ceased to boast about his many voyages around Europe and his expertise as a navigator. Many influential men knew him. At one time, he led many to believe that he had explored Iceland, which was called "Thule" in those days. He told tales of how he and his crew had arrived just after the ice had melted. Researchers now doubt this tale was true, but as advertisers know, exaggeration often makes a sale.

Columbus wasn't an accomplished mathematician or scientist. Much of his knowledge came from reading the *Travels of Marco Polo*, who traveled by land, not by sea. He also conferred with some of the educated men of the day in Lisbon, such as Regiomontanus, a German astronomer. Even the biblical prophet Esdras (Ezra) predicted that water only covered about one-seventh of the earth's surface. Because the earth was then perceived as a much smaller sphere, a journey across the Atlantic Ocean in wooden sailing ships seemed quite feasible to those who were ambitious. Therefore, Columbus felt he could convince King John II of Portugal to finance a journey to the Indies (India), that fanciful country from which wealth would come.

While Columbus was in Portugal, his wife, Filipa, died. Historians place her death around 1484.

During that same year, Columbus was granted an audience with King John II. The king was interested, but he referred Columbus's proposal to Martin Behaim—an authority on scientific navigation—along with the king's own advisors, "Joseph the Jew" and Diogo Ortiz de Villegas, a bishop. However, using the astrolabe, an instrument intended for navigation, Behaim and the others determined that such a trip wouldn't be successful.

Next, Columbus decided to turn to Spain. Bartholomew was delayed in England, so it was up to Christopher to make a proposal to King Ferdinand II and Queen Isabella.

The Spanish Proposal

In 1492, King Ferdinand had to rush to the front to suppress the Muslims, who were invading southern Spain. Queen Isabella stayed in Cordoba to organize shipments of supplies for the soldiers. While waiting to meet with the monarchs, Columbus met a lovely woman by the name of Beatriz Enríquez de Arana. Although they had an intimate relationship, Columbus never married her. He and Beatriz had a son in 1488, whom they named Fernando. To ensure the boy would not be disinherited, Columbus claimed paternity.

While the queen continued attending to military matters, she was told about Columbus's proposal and was interested. The royal court then moved to city after city, and Columbus was invited to follow. Time passed, but Columbus continued to promote his voyage among the influential elites.

Back in 1487, a Portuguese navigator by the name of Bartholomew Dias was commissioned by Portugal to establish a sea route to India. He and his three caravels left Lisbon, sailed around the Cape of Good Hope at the tip of Africa, and then turned north. However, the crew refused to continue because of the vigorous storms, and Dias was forced to turn back.

Even though Dias hadn't quite reached the Indies and Cathay (China), he was celebrated at the Portuguese court. Word of Dias's voyage reached Queen Isabella, and she was concerned that Portugal would be the first European country to reach India via the sea (for years, Spain and Portugal had competed for the wealth of India). Then the queen remembered Columbus's proposal. However, advised by her confessor not to accept it, she initially decided against it. Religious people of note often had their own preferred priest or "confessor" to whom they communicated in private. Her husband, King Ferdinand, was ambivalent as well since it would be costly.

Next, Columbus considered taking the proposal to France. He took his elder son, Diego, with him and journeyed on foot through Spain toward southern France. In the port city of Palos in Spain, they stopped at an old convent, the Friary of La Rábida, to ask for food and lodging. At that time, it was being used by an order of Franciscan brothers. There he met Prior Juan Perez, who was fascinated by Columbus's proposal and felt it would be a loss for Spain if the plan were awarded to France. Perez asked Columbus to tarry there while he contacted Doctor Garcia Hernandez, an expert in cosmography and astronomy, to promote his proposal. The two of them believed that the plan was indeed feasible and indicated they would meet with the queen again on his behalf.

In 1492, word reached Columbus from Queen Isabella herself that he must return. The last Moorish king had just surrendered in Granada, so the king and queen were in good spirits. The royal couple was presented with arguments in favor of Christopher Columbus's voyage, bolstered by the support of Cardinal Pierre d'Ailly, who was known to be a wise and educated man.

The king and queen then accepted Columbus's proposal. His son Diego was accepted at court as a page to the queen's son, Prince Juan. Christopher's lady friend, Beatriz, traveled from Italy to care for Fernando and saw to it that the boy attended school.

Columbus's Bold Demands

Columbus was a wise man. He knew that, if he was successful, he might be forgotten in the excitement and end his life in poverty. To ensure that wouldn't happen, he presented some outrageous demands to the sovereigns, figuring that some, if not all, might be accepted.

First, Columbus insisted on being named "Admiral of the Ocean Sea" and "High Admiral of Castile." He also wanted one-tenth of the profits from his future discoveries. Still steeped in their success with the Moors, the royal couple agreed.

However, because of the campaign against the Moors, Spain didn't have much capital with which to fund Columbus. His initial sponsor, the Duke of Medina, contributed some money for the journey. As for ships, the city of Palos was required to provide the Crown with vessels because of a past offense, and these vessels would be made available to Columbus by royal decree. The king and queen also gave Columbus permission to impress sailors to man the ships. His first three men were brothers from the well-known Pinzón family. Martín Alonso Pinzón, Francisco Pinzón, and Vincente Yáñez Pinzón were pilots themselves and intensely interested in turning a profit by accompanying Columbus. The largest ship, the *Santa María*, was to be piloted by Columbus. The *Niña*, so-named after Juan Niño of Moguer, was piloted by Vincenti Pinzón, and the *Pinta* was commanded by their brother, Martín, with Francisco as his first mate.

As the men were outfitting the ships, they discovered the *Pinta* had been left in dry dock for too long and needed to be re-caulked. Gear from the ship was also missing, possibly stolen, and needed to be replaced. For staff, Columbus took two barbers, a physician, a secretary, a silversmith, an assayer, and an interpreter. Columbus most likely had a lodestone compass and a 1490 sea chart, which didn't include the then-unknown Pacific Ocean. However, the map would have shown Cipango (Japan).

On August 3, 1492, Columbus left and headed into the mysterious Atlantic. As described by the medieval Arab writer, Xerif al Edrisi, "The ocean encircles the ultimate bounds of the inhabited world and all beyond it is unknown."

Chapter 2 – Dead Reckoning Forward

Looking out from the wooden deck of a sailing ship in the 15th century, one would find no physical points of reference. The traditional method of determining one's position on the sea was called "dead reckoning." A vessel's position was determined by three variables: point of origin, speed, and time. Columbus was an expert with dead reckoning. On the way west, Columbus had the trade winds to his back. Scholars of the time agreed that, in a good wind, a vessel could average between four and a half to six knots. On days when there was little wind, mariners assumed they could travel one to three knots. The only reference Columbus had for the time was an hourglass. At night, he used the North Star, Polaris, as a stable point from which to measure distance. For delineating angular distance from Polaris, Columbus used the astrolabe, which was invented in Greece.

No one knows what maps and projected figures Columbus used as references for his journey. Most historians agree he probably used several sources, including Ptolemy's estimate from 140 CE; that of Persian geographer Ahmad al-Farghani, who lived from 798 to 861 CE; and a map created by Marinus of Tyre, a Phoenician who lived in

Greece between 70 and 130 CE. Columbus used the circumference of the earth as a basis for predicting the width of the Atlantic Ocean. In his interpretation of al-Farghani's figure about the earth's circumference, Columbus miscalculated the distance he needed to travel by using the Roman mile as a basis rather than the Arab mile used by the geographer. Therefore, he mistakenly surmised that the earth's circumference was 16,305 nautical miles rather than 24,000 miles, which was much more accurate. He also miscalculated the longitude and latitude of Cipango (Japan). Columbus's estimates were mostly built on faulty assumptions, but so were the other prevailing beliefs of his day.

First Stop

On August 6, 1492, a shout was heard from the *Pinta*. The ship seemed to be foundering near Lanzarote Island, northeast of the Canary Islands. From the windy shore, the captain, Martín Pinzón, shouted to Admiral Columbus that the rudder was broken and the ship was taking on water. Rumor had it that the ship had been sabotaged by its owners, Cristóbal Quintero and Gomes Rascon, out of resentment for being required to surrender their ships for royal use.

Pinzón was a resourceful man and quite ingenious, so he and his men jerry-rigged a substitute and then nursed the *Pinta* to Gran Canaria Island. Columbus, who was aboard the *Pinta*, tried to secure another vessel, but none was available. Realizing he had to use the *Pinta*, he purchased a new rudder, and his men put it on. In the meantime, the *Niña* and *Santa María* sailed to nearby Gomero Island to wait for the repair to be completed.

While docked, Columbus saw the volcano on Tenerife Island spew smoke and fire. An eruption was imminent, and a month had already passed, so they didn't want to tarry any longer. Hurriedly, they packed water, meat, wood, and ancillary supplies. The days were very calm—the devious calmness that usually precedes a storm. On September 6, 1492, they quickly departed Gomero.

In the middle of the night on September 8, great waves leaped over the bow like giant tongues. The ships veered to the northeast due to the wind, and Columbus kept ranting to his men to tack the sails so they could steer to the west. Otherwise, they would end up in the North Atlantic.

Deceptions

Columbus's original logs were lost to history, but a copy was made in 1493 called the "Barcelona Copy." Bartolomé de las Casas, a Dominican historian, received this copy and used it in his own history of Columbus, which he wrote in 1530. De la Casas reported that Columbus sensed the fear and trepidation of his men, and he said Columbus kept two sets of distance figures in his logs, with one that deliberately underestimated the actual distances traveled per day to help put the sailors' minds at ease once they lost sight of land. On the first day that the blue sky and blue water were all they could see around them, Columbus reported that many shed tears. On September 10, he told them they'd only traveled two and a half leagues when, in fact, they'd sailed forty-eight leagues. Columbus did this throughout the journey but made accurate notes elsewhere for history's sake.

His men also became somewhat alarmed when they noted that north on the compass wasn't aligned perfectly with the North Star. He explained to the men what astronomers and mariners have known for years—the North Star isn't situated exactly due magnetic north, as shown on a compass. Because of the tilt of the earth on its axis, it will lie to one side or the other, depending upon the month and time of year. This phenomenon is called precession. Sailors in the 15th century didn't understand it fully but knew of it, so Columbus told his men to expect a "slight variation."

Hints of Flora and Fauna

The men were excited when, on September 14, they sighted a tern and a boatswain bird. Terns generally fly no more than eighty-six miles from shore and are known for accompanying boats on long ferry journeys across bays, hoping to be thrown some tidbits from passengers. A boatswain is a tropical bird, and it most likely came from the Cape Verde Islands off the western coast of Africa.

The seamen also excitedly reported seeing tufts of grass on September 16. Some thought this meant they were near the mainland, but Columbus patiently explained that the grass was no doubt from some uncharted island.

On September 17, they caught a fish off the deck of the *Santa María*. In addition, they saw herbs floating in the water. The admiral said it came from the west "in which direction, I trust in that high God in whose hands are all victories, we shall sight land." On the 20th and the 21st of the month, several booby birds (most likely booby gannets, which fly around the South Atlantic) landed on the *Pinta*, where they roosted for a while.

Fear Sets In

The seamen, including Columbus, had never been to sea for nearly a month without spotting land. The sea was eerily calm toward the end of September, so they had to keep tacking their sails to try to catch what little wind there was. The sea rose in great swells such as they had never seen, and it was unnerving trying to guide the ships so they wouldn't capsize by taking the waves broadside. They had made less progress than Columbus had anticipated, and—given the miscalculations he had started out with—he was becoming concerned. He knew he couldn't show this attitude to the sailors, however.

The crew became restless and started to complain at that point, thinking they should turn back and return to Spain. Thankfully, the winds picked up again, and they moved further westward at a faster rate. Columbus was relieved when he knew they had picked up the trade winds. Martín Pinzón and Columbus exchanged sea charts, and they determined that they were now 2,200 miles west of the Canary Islands. Columbus himself was astonished since he had only calculated that the entire journey would be about 1,700 miles.

Coming of the Sandpipers and the Dorados

On September 25, the crew saw numerous sandpipers, shorebirds that race in and out of surf snatching baby crabs, sea snails, and tiny fish. Finally, Columbus heard the call he had so fervently anticipated: "Land Ahoy!" Martín Alonzo climbed up to the poop and thought he saw it, too, lying on the distant horizon. One by one, other sailors rushed up the masts to look.

Several dorados swam by, and the men caught some of them for food. Dorados, also known as dolphin fish or mahi-mahi, are native to the Caribbean Islands. The sailors were joyous, and many bathed in the sea.

Disappointment soon set in, though. As the three vessels sailed west, drifting somewhat southwest, it was determined the seamen had mistaken a large cloudbank for land in the distance.

On October 1, Columbus continued deliberately underestimating the distance traveled so as not to panic the sailors. He told them they had traveled about 2,000 nautical miles, but in truth, they had come 2,404 nautical miles.

It is noteworthy that he drifted southward because the winds had shifted. It was clear that there were many islands nearby since the seamen noticed not only sandpipers but also flying fish. Flying fish swim near the waterline of ships and leap out of the water to snatch the smaller fish churned up by the speed of the vessel. The Pinzón brothers expected to come upon the islands of Cipango (Japan), and they complained when Cipango wasn't sighted. The sailors also muttered, but the discussions accelerated into arguments.

By October 6, Martín Alonso's hesitation fomented talks of mutiny. Alonso was particularly agitated because he believed they had missed Japan. He attempted to then get Columbus to turn south since he thought doing so would give them a greater chance of landing in Cathay (China) and then continuing along the coast further south and southwest to get to the Indies. Columbus insisted, though, that they sail west. Had he not done so, they would have ended up in the South Atlantic.

Follow the Birds!

The Portuguese, who were known as the world's most accomplished sailors, have a history of finding land by following flocks of birds. On October 7, the crew of the *Pinta* reported that they'd sighted huge flocks of birds flying west/southwest. Columbus immediately had the ships change course in that direction. He noted, too, that the weeds seen floating on the sea were fresh and green, which meant land was close by. In addition, the men saw terns, boobies, and even ducks. Night birds were singing their melodious songs, and it was well-known that such birds only sing when perched on a solid surface such as a tree branch. Hope was high among the men.

Suddenly, their optimism was squelched when the sea went empty again, bereft of any signs of landed life. They muttered and complained loudly once again. Columbus attempted to quiet them down with promises of wealth and jewels beyond their imaginings. He had done that before—too many times. This time, it wasn't working. On October 10, strident arguments broke out, and the crew seriously considered throwing Columbus overboard. Contemporary historian, Peter Martyr, remarked, "After the thirtieth day, roused by madness, they declared they were going back."

On October 11, the men on the *Pinta* screamed out that they saw a cane and an object made of iron floating in the sea. Then the men on deck saw a land plant with berries on it, floating along with a small board. It was nighttime, and the sailors started to wake each other up. Columbus was on the quarter-deck and saw a light too small to be identified. Rodrigo de Triana, one of the sailors, then said he saw a light, and Columbus called to Pedro Gutierrez, a "gentleman of the king's bedchamber." Columbus thought it was the flickering light of a candle. At two in the morning on October 12, 1492, a sailor by the name of Rodrigo de Triana raced up the mast in the blackness of night, looked out at the sea to the west, and bellowed, "Land Ahoy!" Whoever saw land first was promised a silk doublet and 10,000 maravedis annually, which would come to about $600 per year.

Land Ahoy!

The next morning, they touched land. The sailors gathered on their respective decks and sang the church hymn "Salve Regina." Columbus then had two flags hoisted on each ship. One flag had a crown and an "F" on it for King Ferdinand, and the other had a crown and "Y" on it for "Ysabel," that is, Queen Isabella. Columbus then claimed the land in the name of the king and queen and planted a cross.

The land was an island named "Las Casas" in the Lucayan Archipelago, of which the Bahamas is a part. Some historians indicate it was Watling's Island, an island of the Bahamas. This island was later named San Salvador Island in honor of Columbus's landing site.

Chapter 3 – Initial Exploration

Columbus and his crew believed this place was the Indies. They were somewhat surprised, therefore, when they met the indigenous people of this place. In Columbus's words, "They appeared to be a race of people very poor in everything. They go as naked as when their mothers bore them." The indigenous population called this place "Guanahani," and Columbus called them "Indians" because he thought he had reached India.

Columbus further described the natives, whom we now identify as members of the Taíno, Lucayan, and Arawak tribes, as strong and handsome people who had brown skin and short, coarse hair, with some longer strands tied at the back. Some painted themselves in colors—red, black, or white—and others wore gold nose rings. The sailors gifted them with glass beads, red caps, and trinkets. The natives then brought the men parrots, skeins of cotton, darts, javelins, and other incidentals.

On the following day, the people of the island came over to the ships in long and slender boats made from the trunks of trees. Each large canoe could carry forty or more men, and there were smaller canoes as well. They excitedly boarded Columbus's ship and admired the items they saw aboard.

Investigators later discovered that the one-log canoes were most likely made from the ceiba tree, native to Mexico and South America. The ceiba tree can grow as high as 230 feet.

The Search for Gold

Having heard stories about the gold and jewels the Europeans had acquired from the Indies, Columbus and his men pointed out the people's jewelry and made gestures to indicate they wanted to know where there was more gold. With the help of a translator, the mariners ascertained some elements of the natives' language and determined that they had suggested going to the south and southwest—but not the northwest. The natives told them the people who inhabited the islands in the northwest were hostile.

Columbus decided to set off in that direction the next day. Before doing so, he captured a few of his guests and took them on board to guide him to the source of the gold. Columbus docked near the island they indicated, which was heavily forested and fertile. He then sent out a few sailors to explore it, and they reported there was a large lake in the center of the island. They saw no gold deposits and no gold dust in the streamlets.

The people at that new island were kind and very much like the natives Columbus had encountered on his first stop. They also offered Columbus and the men trinkets like the ones they were given at the prior island. Columbus visited several more islands and was given fruit and some unidentified greens. Again, canoes came alongside the European ships. Seeing that he had a chance to escape, one of the natives who had been forcibly held by Columbus leaped into the sea, boarded a canoe, and rapidly sailed to shore. More jumped off and swam like fish to the shore. Columbus reported that "they all fled like hens" into the woods. To make amends for having seized the natives earlier, Columbus prepared some food and left trinkets on the beach for them.

On one of the islands they sighted, the sailors were astonished when the people kneeled down and shouted out greetings from the shore. Columbus continued to explore the many islands he came across but didn't dock at all of them.

There was a larger island in the archipelago, and Columbus docked there. He called the island "Santa María de la Concepción." When he asked the indigenous about gold, the people told Columbus that there were some tribes that not only wore earrings but also had wide armbands of gold. One of the men asked that Columbus take him to another island, but it wasn't the island where gold was said to be found. The man guided him there, and Columbus named it Fernandina Island after the king.

The seamen explored Fernandina Island more thoroughly, as it was larger. Columbus was awed by the luscious foliage of the many trees and plants. He also noted the brightly-colored fish in the shallows. The natives then indicated there was yet another island that had gold. Columbus discovered that the people who lived there were somewhat more civilized. They weren't naked but wore some clothing. He again asked about the gold, and several volunteered to take him to yet another island to the southeast. The natives called it "Samoet," but Columbus renamed it "Isabela" after the queen. It corresponds to Fortune Island in the Bahamas.

Villages

There were small villages on those islands. They were well-built and had tall chimneys. The houses, which they called *bohíos*, had sparse furniture mostly made of netting, and their beds were like hammocks. The islands were rich and fertile. Because Europeans marveled about the spices from the Indies, Columbus wrote in his diary, "I believe there are in them many herbs and many trees which are of great value in Spain for dyes and for medicines of spicery."

As the explorers went to various islands, they gathered samples. Columbus also killed a large serpent and skinned it, taking the snakeskin aboard as a gift for the queen. The villagers were friendly and went to the interior of the islands to obtained fresh water for the sailors.

In speaking with the people, Columbus heard of a larger island and left again in search of gold. The natives they had met so far had small pieces of it adorning themselves, but Columbus remarked that they were "poor in gold." In a letter for the Spanish king and queen, Columbus promised that, on many of the islands, "there was gold and spices."

Cuba

Based on 15th-century maps, which failed to account for the entire American continent, Columbus thought the large island toward which he was headed was Cipango (Japan). He reached this island, which was actually Cuba, on October 28. The fishermen they encountered were timid and fled upon his arrival. He described the palm trees and the mountains he saw in the distance. "This island," he wrote, "is the most beautiful that eyes have seen, full of good harbors and deep rivers, and the sea appears as if it never rose." He sailed along the northeast coast of Cuba. Knowing Columbus was interested in gold, which they called *mucay*, the people kept promising he would find gold on yet another island.

One of the island guides told Columbus that the people of the next island beat the gold into blocks like ingots. He spoke of a rich king who was located a four days' journey from there, and Columbus planned to meet him.

On November 6, they docked at a bay and located a large village. The people greeted them, knelt at their feet, and kissed them. Columbus and his sailors were escorted to a large house, and the people made a grand meal for them. They also smoked an herb in cigarettes made from rolled-up leaves. It seems it was not tobacco because it made the people drowsy, and they acted as if they were drunk. The people had small farms on which they raised beans, yams, and corn. In separate fields, they grew cotton, mostly used to make fishing nets and clothing. Columbus asked about pepper, as that was a valued spice from the Indies. The people brought him what is called *ají*, or chili pepper.

Without permission, Martín Alonso Pinzón left the *Santa María* and *Niña* and took the *Pinta* northeast in search of gold. Pinzón had been told by the natives that an island called "Babeque" or "Beneque" contained gold. He explored the island and several other small islands but found no gold.

Hispaniola

Columbus landed on another island on December 5, 1492, and named the island "Hispaniola." This island is modern-day Haiti and the Dominican Republic.

The people—Taíno Indians and the Arawak tribes—greeted them warmly. Columbus wrote in his log that these people were gentle and could be converted to Christianity, as that was one of the goals Catholic Spain considered essential in colonization.

The islands were rich in crabs and shellfish. He described one crab as enormous and had it salted to preserve it on the journey home. There were also oysters, and the men opened a great many of them in search of pearls to bring back to the Spanish sovereigns. None had pearls.

Further inland, there were tall, sturdy oak trees, which the men cut down to use as masts since the one on the *Niña* was well-weathered and wind-beaten. Columbus sailed in and out of the many capes he saw there. Most of the people who lived in these areas fled when the men landed. Some of the islands had rivers, which they explored. There were groves of trees alongside many of the glittering beaches, and inland, there were huge pine trees. Noting the size of Hispaniola, Columbus knew he wouldn't have time to explore all of it, but he wrote in his journal that he had no doubt there were many precious stones that could be mined. Columbus kidnapped several indigenous people from Hispaniola and some of the smaller islands to take back to Spain.

Some of the Spanish who had accompanied Columbus settled in a town Columbus called "La Isabela." There were rumors that gold could be found there, but it was also a fertile area suitable for farming.

Columbus moved around the western coast of Hispaniola, docking here and there to explore different areas of the island. The Taíno were always sure to indicate where gold might be found, as that seemed to please Columbus. There were many villages on the shores of the island, each with its own chief. The people often spoke of a tribe that apparently lived northeast of the island, called "Caribs." Those people, the natives indicated, were extremely hostile. The indigenous on board the ship begged Columbus for protection from the Caribs.

The Caribs may have been cannibals. Cannibals believed that if they consumed the meat of their enemies, they would gain their enemies' strength. Ethnologists indicate that the Caribs did populate some of the islands just east of Hispaniola.

Wreck of the *Santa María*

On the eve of Christmas Day, Columbus retired to his cabin. One of his sailors brought the *Santa María* toward the shore, while the *Niña* pulled up nearby. The sea was as still as glass. Unbeknownst to Columbus, however, the sailor turned the helm of the *Santa María* over to a cabin boy, which was against Columbus's policy. When the tide changed, the ship suddenly slid up onto a sandbank and started to list to the left. When he realized what had happened, Columbus came rushing out of his cabin, along with the ship's master. The other men raced above deck, and some of them boarded the *Niña* in a panic. When the tide came in, the water rose rapidly around the *Santa María*, but the ship was still jammed into the sandbank. Columbus ordered the crew to lighten the ship by cutting off the masts, hoping the ship would break loose. It didn't. Timbers from the hull split off, and the *Santa María* leaned leeward and tilted into the sea. The men tried to gather up the goods and materials they could salvage from the wreck.

Columbus then boarded the *Niña* himself to make arrangements for his men to bed there for the night. The natives from the nearby village gathered about in their canoes, and its *cacique* (king) hastened to bring the men into the village. The king, whose name was Guacanagarí, was very compassionate. He directed his people to help collect what goods they could from the ship and bring them to Columbus for safekeeping. Of him, Columbus said, "So honest [are] they, without any covetousness for the goods of others, and so above all, he was a virtuous king." Guacanagarí then offered Columbus some food and shelter, all the while assuring him that he and his men would be well taken care of in their village.

Then the Gold

The following day, some of the native men brought Columbus pieces of gold, which they exchanged for little hawk bells. These were small, round bells made of bronze, such as one might see hung from a string of hemp at Christmas. Guacanagarí told Columbus to travel with some of the villagers, who showed him a primitive gold mine there. The natives themselves agreed to gather up as much gold as they could find, and Columbus could take it home to Spain.

Columbus dined Guacanagarí aboard the *Niña*, and he was impressed with the caravel. In addition, Columbus demonstrated some of their arms, including bows and arrows. Then he shot off one of his cannons. All the natives were shocked at the loud noise and fell to the ground, astonished at its power. The people again mentioned their enemies, the Caribs, and asked Columbus to protect them from a possible attack. The king awarded Columbus with an ornate mask that had gold eyes and golden ornamentation.

Columbus built a fortress on the island by cannibalizing parts from the *Santa María*. He called the port where it was located La Navidad. There, he left twenty-one of his own men, along with supplies, and tasked them with creating a settlement. He also left a small herd of cattle from the cargo hold to reproduce and provide meat and milk. Then he instructed his men to expand the gold mine and bid them goodbye. Columbus planned on returning the following year, hoping to see a storehouse of gold and goods.

The *Pinta* Arrives

Columbus then followed the northern coast of Hispaniola, and on January 6, 1493, he spotted the *Pinta* approaching from the northwest. His conversation with his disobedient colleague, Martín Alonso Pinzón, was brief, as he didn't want to show any anger in front of the natives. Pinzón then gave Columbus some of the gold for which he had traded trinkets. In terms of size and quality, the pieces were like those Columbus and his men had obtained. Martín informed Columbus that some of the natives said there were yet two more islands to the east with gold.

Departure

On January 10, Columbus went aboard the *Niña*, and they set sail, steering northeast to cross the Atlantic. They stopped at a small island, where they were greeted with a mixed reception: the natives were cautiously friendly but armed with bows and arrows. The men made their usual exchange of trinkets. Then, suddenly, a group of naked natives came tearing out from behind some trees and rushed at Columbus and his men. The Spanish drew their swords and fought back. One native was slashed in the buttocks, another in his chest. Perhaps these were the Caribs about whom the islanders had warned them.

It wasn't a vicious fight, but Columbus became concerned about the men he had left behind at the fortress La Navidad. He visited another island, where he noted that the men had weapons that were somewhat more advanced. However, the natives were gracious and gave them food to eat.

They then set sail east/northeast on to the great Atlantic, where only blue met blue on the horizon. They plotted a course toward the Azores, off the western coast of Portugal. On February 7, Columbus estimated he was about 220 miles west of the Azores.

By February 10, they found themselves headed toward the western African coast and turned northward. On February 12, the seas were turbulent, and a great storm hit them the following day. As the sea swells towered many feet in the air, the men had to scramble to ensure the mainsail was "close-reefed," or mostly folded so it would catch the wind. On the 13th and 14th, the crew reported that they had to "run before the wind," meaning the winds were driving them forward. They could easily be driven off course, and the rudder alone couldn't compensate. The *Pinta* was separated from the *Niña*, and the two ships lost sight of each other despite the lanterns hanging in their windows. The crew prayed and made pledges to go on pilgrimages of thanksgiving if they made it home alive.

The Azores!

On Monday, February 18, Columbus reached the island of Santa Maria in the Azores. Several sailors discovered from the inhabitants that there was a shrine, so they visited it to give thanks. However, without warning, several armed men grabbed the sailors and arrested them. They then approached the *Niña* and demanded to board it, but the sailors adamantly refused. The men represented João Castenheira, the governor of the island, who accused Columbus of failing to obtain official permission to land there.

Columbus told them he had written proof from the king and queen of Spain, along with letters of recommendation from other dignitaries. He added that he carried the title "Admiral of the Ocean Sea," but, of course, they had never heard of the title. They didn't know who Columbus was, nor did they care. He and the armed guards stood on their respective decks, hollering back and forth amid the crash of the waves. Columbus demanded the release of his men held on land.

The guards questioned the men at great length, trying to pry out confessions of piracy. Because they hadn't been able to arrest Columbus, they let the men return to the *Niña.*

After this unfortunate incident, Columbus concluded that relations between Portugal and Spain had gone sour. There was no doubt about the nationality of Columbus's men due to their dress and dialect.

He pulled out of that port and found a smaller port, that of San Miguel, where he could make some repairs and fill his casks for ballast. It was now February 21. One day, several men approached the *Niña*. Five claimed to be sailors, another claimed to be a notary, and the last one a priest. Columbus treated them courteously and showed them his papers but never made himself accessible, lest they arrest him. Columbus then left the port and sailed north. He planned on going directly to Spain, but another storm delayed him, and he was forced to dock in Lisbon, Portugal.

The locals told him that many ships had been lost in the storm. Columbus then sent a letter to King John II of Portugal. On March 5, they met at Vale do Paraiso hostel just north of Lisbon. It was a cordial but rather stilted meeting. Columbus was correct in his assumption that relations between Lisbon and Spain weren't friendly at that time. The king stiffly informed Columbus he had broken the Treaty of Alcáçovas, signed in 1479, by which Spain agreed not to colonize any islands off the eastern coast of Africa except for the Canary Islands, which Spain controlled. Columbus insisted he hadn't violated the treaty.

The People's Reception

Once the word about Columbus's remarkable journey got out to the sailors on shore, the news traveled quickly. Crowds gathered by his ship with cheering, trumpets, and drums. Columbus brought out some of the natives he had on board, with their feathers and painted faces. Agents and priests came out to greet the men.

The King Meets Columbus Again

Columbus then finally received a proper reception from King John II. They celebrated mass together, and the king offered to give him any supplies or assistance he needed on his journey back to Spain. He assigned a pilot to help him, along with a mule, and some letters intended for King Ferdinand of Spain. Columbus asked about Queen Isabella of Castile, and she graciously met with him. Bartholomew Dias, the Portuguese explorer who had sailed around Africa and back to Portugal in 1488, met with Columbus, and they shared stories about their adventures.

Illness

Columbus became ill at the end of his first voyage. From what historians can gather from old documents, he allegedly suffered from gout, a painful inflammation caused by a buildup of uric acid in the body. Other researchers, however, claim he had a condition known as reactive arthritis. Both conditions are chronic, and they, no doubt, affected him the remainder of his life.

Arrival in Spain

Columbus met with King Ferdinand and Queen Isabella of Spain on March 15, 1493, in Barcelona. They feasted him and his men, and there were parades in the streets with bands and banners.

Columbus showed the sovereigns samples of what he and his men had gathered. Among the items were chili pepper, gold nuggets, cotton, and the snakeskin from the serpent he had killed on one of the islands. He also had rhubarb, raw cinnamon, golden jewelry the Taíno wore, and the gold mask from the native king. He spoke highly of Hispaniola, saying there were "mountains and hills, plains and pastures which are fertile" and referenced the notion that there was much more gold for future exploration. As a matter of fact, Hispaniola became a site for future gold mines, but the bounty they had seen so far wasn't as spectacular as he had described.

Columbus suggested they start out with several thousand colonists mining for gold and shipping it to Spain, sending other goods to Europe, and building churches to convert the so-called Indians. The king and queen told him to "treat the Indians very well and lovingly and abstain from doing them any injury."

The Treaty of Discontent

During the 15th century, the Catholic popes held temporal power because there were many countries in Europe in which Catholicism was the state religion, including Spain and Portugal. This meant Spain was obligated to proselytize and bring Christianity to the land Columbus had discovered. When there were international issues, European countries often approached the pope to resolve them.

Following Columbus's arrival, Pope Alexander VI issued an order that placed a north-south line of demarcation through the Atlantic, indicating the lands lying west of the line were open for Spanish colonization, while lands east of the line were the property of Portugal. This was known as the Treaty of Tordesillas, and it was signed in 1494. Despite signing the treaty, Portugal contested it, and the position of the line was altered in 1500 when the Portuguese explorer, Pedro Cabral, landed in South America in what is now Brazil. He claimed it for Portugal.

The Treaty of Tordesillas was always brought up whenever there were disagreements about the lands colonized after 1493. However, other than cases regarding boundaries, the treaty was mostly ignored.

Great Expectations

Word of Columbus's discoveries raced around Europe. Although Columbus hadn't discovered the treasure of the Far East, Spain and Portugal craved the wealth they could harvest from colonization. There were intrigues and carefully laid out schemes to be the first nation to settle there. The meager samples Columbus had brought back to King Ferdinand and Queen Isabella served only to whet their appetites for imagined power and possessions in the New World. Thus, Columbus was commissioned to return to the New World.

Chapter 4 – Second Voyage

The Tribute System

During the summer of 1493, Spain built and outfitted fourteen caravels and three *barques*, including the *Niña*. Each had a low draught (shorter keel) for navigating the rivers in Hispaniola. Two thousand people, mostly volunteers, were to accompany Columbus. Many of them were wealthy young men in search of adventure, but they were unaccustomed to hard work. Columbus didn't have a full complement of craftsmen and farmers, who would have been more useful. Most of the vessels had over one hundred passengers each, intended to be the foundation of Spanish settlements.

The Tribute System

Spain planned on creating an empire of sorts in the Indies. The passengers who left with Christopher Columbus were required to produce a set amount of gold or goods that could be sent back to Spain. They would use the natives to help them and—in exchange—the natives could split the profits among themselves. For their tribute, the indigenous population was expected to contribute twenty-five pounds of gold or cotton.

Among Columbus's passengers were Alonso de Ojeda, Peter Martyr, Pedro Margarite, Friar Bernardo Buil, Michele da Cuneo,

Ponce de León, and Pedro de Las Casas. Michele da Cuneo was a childhood friend of Columbus from Savona, Italy. Alonso de Ojeda was the brother of the Grand Inquisitor of Spain, who was acquainted with techniques of investigation. Friar Buil was a papal representative; Ponce de León was an explorer who later discovered Florida; Pedro Las Casas and Peter Martyr were both chroniclers.

Besides long-lasting food and supplies, Columbus was entrusted with vegetable seeds to plant on the island of Hispaniola. In addition, he took an assortment of domestic animals and agricultural equipment.

In 1493, Columbus left Cadiz, Spain. The trade winds were kind on this voyage, and Columbus had to deal with only one hurricane. He landed initially on the Caribbean islands of the Antilles, also called the windward and leeward islands. The windward islands were those favorable to the trade winds when going from east to west, while the leeward islands were those that handled the trade winds that blew in the opposite direction.

Most of the islands Columbus visited this time were different than those he recorded during his first voyage. He named these islands, and many bear the same names today—Montserrat, Antigua, Redonda, Nevis, Guadalupe, Dominica, St. Kitts, and the Virgin Islands.

Cannibals of Dominica

Southeast of the island of Guadalupe was an island he named "Dominica." He and his men found evidence that the indigenous people there were cannibals: human skulls and fragments of human bones lying about. The natives of Guadalupe did come out to greet the sailors, but with great caution. Columbus reported that they were ethnically similar to those he'd seen before. He later discovered that the Caribs, who populated Dominica, captured men from the Arawak tribe and consumed their flesh. Women weren't consumed but used as concubines, and boys were used as laborers until they came of age, at which time they were eaten. The Caribs managed to eradicate most of the Arawak either through cannibalism or intermarriage. They then turned to neighboring islands.

Puerto Rico

Upon his arrival in today's Puerto Rico, Columbus named it "San Juan Bautista" after St. John the Baptist, a Catholic saint. The Puerto Rican population consisted mostly of the Taíno tribe, whom Columbus had met on Hispaniola during his first voyage. They had been settlers there for thousands of years and called this island "Borinquen." Columbus found the Taíno peacefully engaged in farming.

It is interesting to note that the Taíno people raised cassava root, a starchy vegetable with a high carbohydrate level, as well as pineapples and sweet potatoes. Shellfish provided them with protein, but their diet was limited to these crops.

Cuba

Columbus explored Cuba more thoroughly this time, focusing on the southern coast, sailing in and out of its many capes. On one occasion, he dispatched Alonso de Ojeda with fifteen other men to explore the land in search of gold. Upon their return, they reported that they hadn't found any deposits, but many of the natives panned for gold in the streams and found some gold nuggets.

Although the explorers were pleased with this find, they had entertained dreams of finding a great deal of gold. It was disappointing when they realized that mining for gold would be laborious and expensive.

In July of 1493, toward the end of the Cuban exploration, Columbus wrote about a violent storm near Cape Cruz that was "so sudden, violent, and with such a downpour of rain that the deck was underwater." The sailors had to man the pumps for nearly four days to prevent the ship from sinking. He also reported that rations were low, and even the biscuits they brought with them were rotten. When the storm finally passed, Columbus visited the island of Jamaica.

Jamaica

At Jamaica, Columbus was greeted by villagers who shouted "Almirante," which means admiral. Word about Columbus had gotten around the Indies, and most islanders knew of him. They were mostly naked, but their king wore gold ornaments made of a gold alloy called *guanín*.

In the distance rose the Blue Mountains that indeed looked blue, as Columbus described. In addition, there were many species of birds he'd never seen before. Next, he was anxious to return to Hispaniola to visit the settlement he had founded during his first voyage.

Hispaniola

On November 22, 1493, Columbus visited Hispaniola and was deeply distressed by what he saw. The fort he had built at La Navidad had been destroyed. When he and his crew investigated, they found human bones and the bodies of eleven of the thirty-nine Spanish settlers he had left behind to colonize the area.

He didn't suspect Guacanagarí, whom he had befriended on his first journey, but sensed it might have been the Caribs. He later discovered that it wasn't the Caribs who had been at fault, but another chieftain from the native Taíno tribe.

There was also substantial evidence of many wars on the island. The farms the men had planted had been neglected, the natives he met appeared to be hungry and ill, and many of their villages were deserted.

Columbus sent out a party of men to explore the heavily-forested regions of the island's interior. When they returned, they reported that there was very little land amenable to farming.

Christopher's brother, Bartholomew, had received funding to travel to the New World and arrived at Hispaniola in 1494. Bartholomew was appointed as the *adelantado*, a senior governor. Bartholomew then founded the city of Santo Domingo, which later became its capital.

Illness

Before reaching the town of La Isabela in Hispaniola, Columbus became ill. His son, Fernando, when he penned Columbus's biography later in life, wrote that he was so ill he was practically comatose: "He had a high fever and drowsiness so that he lost his sight, memory, and other senses." After his traumatic experience at Hispaniola, Columbus was overwrought and had trouble sleeping.

However, Columbus was a tough and determined man, and his passion to be the "Admiral of the Ocean" was stronger than his physical condition. He was about forty-two at the time and, in his own words, admitted, "I attribute my malady to the excessive fatigues and dangers of this voyage: over 27 consecutive years at sea have taken their toll."

Isabella

At the Hispaniola town of La Isabela, Columbus was still unwell, so he rested there before continuing. He then wrote a letter to Queen Isabella of Spain suggesting that the Spanish enslave some of the native population—the Arawak—to farm and mine for gold.

Although the queen firmly refused, Columbus realized he hadn't been keeping up with the expected tributes, so he loaded his ships with 560 Arawak slaves for shipment back to Spain. As it so happened, 200 of them died on the journey back. After the arrival of the healthier ones, the queen arranged to ship these poor unfortunates home to the Indies.

While he was still recovering, Columbus had his men build a fortress called Santo Tomás and placed it under the command of Pedro Margarite, one of his passengers on the voyage. After less than a year, Friar Bernardo Buil came to Columbus to complain about Margarite, saying he was cruel and abusive. He told Columbus that some of the natives had rebelled against Margarite and his men. Columbus's son verified this when he wrote that the settlers went about "inflicting so many injuries upon them that the Indians resolved to avenge themselves."

Margarite Departs

When Margarite discovered that Friar Buil had made accusations against him, he connived to dispel them. However, he failed, and many people became aware of his reputation. In 1495, Margarite gathered a crew, and they took one of the ships back to Spain. Margarite left over three hundred of the initial passengers he traveled with at the town of Vega Real in Hispaniola. It was later reported that these men preyed upon the natives, kidnapped their women, and forced the Taíno into slavery, who hadn't expected this deplorable behavior.

Christopher Columbus Departs

Other Spanish colonists who had settled there were dissatisfied with Columbus, as well, and with the general conditions of the place. Columbus knew he should return with much more gold than he had, so he sought a way to make up for the deficit. It was then he decided to create a slave trade. There would be a ready market for slaves in Seville, Spain. Columbus's childhood friend, Michele de Cuneo, was horrified by this and became very disillusioned. In his journal, de Cuneo said, "The natives tried to escape us, so they sometimes left their infants anywhere on the ground and started to flee like desperate people."

At Beata, a small island nearby, Columbus was met by natives armed with bows that had poisoned arrows, and they told him they had captured some of his men. Columbus managed to calm them down and convince them, with gifts, to release the men. However, bitter feelings fomented. More and more of the natives turned against the Spanish settlers. They attacked them, killing some and forcing the rest back to their ships.

King Guacanagarí, whom Columbus had befriended on his first voyage, was loyal to Columbus and fought against the natives who were killing the Spanish settlers. He and Columbus then gathered together a force of Spanish loyalists and confronted the hostiles outside La Isabela. Columbus and Guacanagari's men attacked the hostile natives with crossbows, and the rebels were forced to retreat into the jungle.

Columbus was a man who was obeyed through fear, not admiration. Most captains had crews that were pressed into service and learned how to use an authoritarian voice when they spoke. The settlers also realized that Columbus had exaggerated his claims about the riches of the New World, which is the downfall of marketeers, and Columbus was a marketeer of his times. Michele de Cuneo, along with many other dissatisfied settlers, demanded that Columbus take them back to Spain. As he was also running out of supplies, Columbus decided to return to Spain, along with those who wanted to go home.

Francisco Roldán was then placed in charge of La Isabela, while Christopher readied himself for the trip home. In 1496, Christopher Columbus returned to Spain.

Chapter 5 – Third Voyage: Chaos Reigns

In 1498, King Ferdinand and Queen Isabella commissioned Columbus to travel to a mainland they had heard about from King John II of Portugal. Supposedly, it lay southwest of the Cape Verde Islands, located about four hundred miles off the coast of western Africa.

In 1498, Columbus departed from Sanlucar, Spain, with six ships. Columbus dispatched three of his ships directly to Hispaniola with long-awaited supplies while he continued south toward the continent of which King John II had spoken. This continent was South America, but the explorers didn't know of the Americas at the time.

When Columbus had explored Cuba on his first and second voyages, he speculated that Cuba must be mainland China. The island, though, didn't match some of the descriptions he'd read, so, in truth, he was probably unsure. When he spotted Hispaniola, he thought the island might be Japan.

Traveling south, he landed on the island of Trinidad. There he came across some natives in their long and narrow canoes. Stopping there, the sailors discovered pearls, all of which they collected to bring back to Spain.

India?

During this voyage, Columbus discovered the coast of South America (what is now Venezuela) near the mouth of the huge Orinoco River. He noted that this was a freshwater river. Therefore, explorers called this land "Terra Firma," or "firm land." Many explorers speculated that a strait leading to the Indian Ocean might lie west of Cuba, but Columbus didn't believe it was the Orinoco since the water was fresh, not salty. He met some of the villagers there, who were only slightly more advanced than the Taíno he had met on the islands. However, they didn't have gold or the rich spices that the Europeans knew came from India, so "Terra Firma" wasn't India.

He didn't present this view after the voyage, however, because he had more pressing business to attend to. He was quite anxious to return to Hispaniola after hearing there had been uprisings and rebellions, including one led by Francisco Roldán, whom he had left in charge along with Bartholomew.

Roldán's Rebellion

When Columbus arrived in Hispaniola, his brother was in Xaragua (Juaragua), trying to deal with Roldán. Ever since he had come to Hispaniola, Roldán had craved control of the entire island—and as many other islands of the West Indies as he could control. In Columbus's absence, he conspired to rid himself of Bartholomew and Diego (also known as Giacomo). Roldán manipulated his supporters by promising to split the wealth of the island with them if they would take the caravel and return to Spain to tell King Ferdinand that Bartholomew was maltreating the indigenous people. Roldán reminded his followers to say that Columbus, Diego, and Bartholomew forced the natives there to erect forts in the overwhelming heat and frequently punished them with severe floggings. Diego was forced to hide so that Roldán's supporters wouldn't capture him.

In truth, the conditions in Hispaniola had vacillated between times of plenty and times of great want. The weather was unpredictable, and the settlers weren't always able to find sufficient amounts of fresh water. On occasion, the settlers' crops had failed, causing hunger and disease. These settlers had mostly come to the Indies hoping to strike it rich but were sorely disappointed.

One of Columbus's passengers, Pedro Las Casas, wrote that, after Columbus's second voyage, Roldán recommended that each settler "have the woman that he wanted, taken from their husbands, or daughters from their fathers, by force or willingly, to use as chambermaids, washerwomen, and cooks, and as many Indian men as they thought necessary to serve them."

Roldán holed up inside the fort of Santo Tomás, waiting for the supplies that were due to come in from Spain. While waiting, he allied himself with two native chieftains who agreed to support him.

When Bartholomew arrived, he met with Roldán to negotiate. Roldán demanded the use of one of the ships to return to Spain. Bartholomew agreed, but Roldán didn't have experienced mariners at his disposal, so he delayed.

Columbus's Ships Arrive

Christopher Columbus's ships arrived with supplies while he was in South America. Captain Sanchez de Carvajal met with Bartholomew Columbus, who apprised him of the situation with Francisco Roldán. De Carvajal and Bartholomew attempted to negotiate with Roldán but were unsuccessful.

Christopher himself arrived in 1498. He was told the situation was so serious that Hispaniola was nearly in a state of anarchy. Realizing there were a tremendous number of rebels, Columbus recognized that the only peaceful solution would be to permit Roldán and his supporters to return to Spain with an experienced crew or—the alternative—relocate himself and his followers to another area of the island. Columbus therefore instructed five ships to accept the Spanish passengers and transport them back to Spain.

On November 16, 1498, Roldán and Christopher signed an agreement to use two ships manned by Spanish seamen to return to Spain. What's more, Columbus was compelled to grant him pardon and to praise Roldán for his services on Hispaniola!

As some of the rebels were at the town of Xaragua, Captain de Carvajal stopped there first to help Roldán's men and their families organize their belongings and make arrangements to leave. It wasn't until January of 1499 that they left for Spain.

On one of those ships, Columbus included a packet of letters addressed to the king and queen. One of the letters, written by Fernando Columbus, spoke about "the damage they (rebels) had done and were continuing to do on the island." He also added that Roldán and his supporters plundered the natives' villages and killed whomever they pleased.

Imprisonment

In 1500, King Ferdinand sent over Francisco de Bobadilla to investigate all the accusations regarding Christopher Columbus, Diego (also known as Giacomo), and Bartholomew. As soon as de Bobadilla's ships showed up, they were met with the sight of two corpses hanging from a gibbet. De Bobadilla was informed that these Spanish settlers had been sentenced to death for rebelling. Bartholomew was in the town of Xaragua at the time, preparing to execute even more men. De Bobadilla's orders were clear. He was to detain whomever he found was guilty, confiscate their goods, and return them to Spain to face trial.

Christopher, Diego, and Bartholomew were then sent back to Spain in shackles aboard the caravel, *La Gorda*, and imprisoned on charges of mismanagement. Much of the testimony presented in court was heavily prejudiced, but not all of it. Among the witnesses was a former settler who reported that Columbus had ordered the nose and ears to be cut off one offender, while another received one hundred lashes for failing to provide Columbus with food for his pantry. Others testified that he had refused food to people who were hungry and was a harsh taskmaster. Historians indicate, however, that these people might have been biased by the fact that they hadn't returned home with the riches they expected.

Friar Buil and Margaret de Cuneo had witnessed the mistreatment of the indigenous population, including beatings and punitive mutilations performed on their bodies. They, no doubt, felt ashamed that such atrocities were perpetrated by those who called themselves Christians.

They and the other settlers said virtually nothing about how they themselves attempted to force the natives to labor in their gold mines and cotton fields. The native people weren't that interested in gold because it was more important for them to work their farms and care for their animals. It puzzled the settlers that they couldn't get the same kind of cooperation from the Hispaniola natives as they received from the commoners at home. The natives were more practical and had less-advanced tools. The Spanish thought of the native people as barbarians, and the natives thought of the Europeans as oppressors.

Columbus had been driven by his own desperation to prove that he had indeed reached China, Japan, and India. He was also under great pressure to return with the valuable tributes he and the other settlers had promised the Crown, but it was clear that he oversold his "product."

As Columbus tried to rationalize the unsatisfactory bounty from the New World, he came to believe that the natives were stubborn and lazy. At one point, he said to the sovereigns, "To prevent my searching for gold the Indians put up as many obstacles as they could." He later modified this, saying that the Indians needed to "return to their plantings because they were starving and dying at an incredible rate." Columbus didn't realize that they died not of starvation but because they lacked immunity to European diseases.

Eventually, Columbus realized that some of the criticisms leveled against him were true and confessed to many, but not all, of the offenses. He then asked for mercy and begged the sovereigns to restore his wealth so that his heirs might be left with enough to sustain themselves.

The king and queen came to the realization that none of the Columbus brothers were good administrators, and much of the criticism they'd heard was prejudiced. They decided that Columbus was never again to serve as the governor of Hispaniola. In 1502, Columbus was replaced by Nicolas de Ovando.

However, because the king and queen recognized Columbus's contribution, they released the three after six weeks. They also saw to it that the property Bombadilla had confiscated from Christopher was returned.

Execution of the Golden Flower Queen

Unfortunately, de Ovando was a very poor administrator, as well. Upon his arrival, he called for an assembly of the Taíno *caciques* to meet him, ostensibly with the intention of establishing a relationship. This was a fabrication. De Ovando wanted to eliminate any possible dissensions during his administration, so he planned on killing the leaders.

One of them was Queen Anacaona. She was revered among her people as a poet and ballad writer. Even today, her images appear in many portraits and paintings about the history of Haiti.

Queen Anacoana was the head of the tribe in Xaragua, in today's western Haiti. Her brother, Bohechio, also a *cacique*, had rebelled against the Spanish settlers who first came to their land in 1495 and was killed by a Spanish soldier when he objected to paying tribute to Spain. However, Anacaona was more interested in making peace with these foreigners, as were all the other leaders who flocked together to meet with this new governor.

She met with de Ovando, as well as about eighty other Taíno leaders. De Ovando invited them into an assembly building.

De Ovando was a suspicious man and a known misogynist. He felt that this beautiful woman was sent by the natives to seduce the men and force them to submit to her. De Ovando then took her, along with the known rebels, and had them stand outside the meeting house while his men set fire to the building, killing every soul inside. Next, he coerced the men to swear false testimony against Anacaona and then sentenced her to be hanged. The rest of the native leaders were also tortured and killed.

Anacaona's story has been embellished upon since then, and she became very much of a legend among the Caribbean people as someone who stood for the rights of her people.

Chapter 6 – The Last Voyage

The "Isthmus of Darien"

When Columbus read of Pedro Álvares Cabral's expedition of 1500, he noted that Cabral had sailed southeast from Portugal across the South Atlantic and landed at Porto Seguro in Brazil. Fellow explorers then speculated that, if one sailed southwest from Portugal, there would be a landmass—an isthmus—through which there would be a strait leading to the Indian Ocean and India. No one knew about the Pacific Ocean at that time. This so-called "isthmus" isn't an isthmus, but rather a segment of land called the Darien Gap, partially located in the province of Darien in Panama.

During his first voyage, Columbus had mistaken Cuba for China, then conjectured there was a landmass to the southwest, and perhaps that was the Isthmus of Darien. During his third voyage, Columbus had sailed southwest. The land he saw appeared to be larger than an isthmus, and the Orinoco River had fresh water.

In May of 1502, Columbus was dispatched to seek out this strait that supposedly cut through an imagined isthmus. He had at his disposal four seaworthy vessels—the *Capitana*, the *Gallega*, the *Vizcaína*, and the *Santiago de Palos*.

Hispaniola

Before seeking out the isthmus, Columbus first wanted to exchange the *Santiago de Palos* for another vessel because it was clumsy and slow, so he stopped at Hispaniola. As he approached the shore, he notified the new governor there, Nicolás de Ovando, regarding an exchange. De Ovando, however, harbored negative feelings toward Columbus and made him anchor in a smaller estuary nearby. He also refused to provide Columbus with another ship, although he did have one available.

When Columbus arrived at the governor's headquarters, de Ovando was preparing to send twenty-eight ships to Spain. As he was a veteran seaman, Columbus warned de Ovando about an approaching storm he had run into on his way to Hispaniola. The governor ignored the warning anyway and dispatched all twenty-eight ships. As it turned out, the storm was a massive hurricane, and de Ovando lost twenty-five of the twenty-eight vessels he sent to Spain. The notorious rebel, Roldán, and Columbus's investigator, Francisco de Bobadilla, were aboard one of the ships and were lost in the storm, along with the gold they carried. It was rumored that most of the gold had been stolen from the natives.

Jamaica

In July, Columbus stopped briefly at the island now called Jamaica. The people he met there seemed familiar. Indeed, they were the Arawak/Taíno tribes he'd met in San Salvador and the Antilles Islands on this first visit.

Honduras

He then sailed for Guanaja, an island off the coast of Honduras in Central America settled by the Payan, a semi-nomadic people who hunted and fished. They also raised cassava, maize, and beans. The island had a plethora of animal life, including wild boars, turkeys, monkeys, and deer. Unlike the Taíno he'd met on the Caribbean islands, these people wore some clothing, although it was scanty.

Columbus then explored the Yucatan Peninsula, current-day Costa Rica, Nicaragua, and Panama.

In Honduras, Columbus's crew met a man who knew something of their language and offered to accompany them on their local expeditions as an interpreter. They were delighted and rewarded him with numerous trinkets and colored cloths.

Several storms blew up unexpectedly in the region, and they raged on and off for two months. The thunderstorms were so intense as to frighten even the most hardened seamen. The sails were torn, and the damage to their vessels was severe. "I have seen many tempests," wrote Columbus, "but none so violent and of such a long duration." While in Costa Rica, there was an unfortunate incident. Columbus had sent out some men in a dinghy to search for food along a river when another tropical storm kicked up without warning. The water suddenly rose like a wall and engulfed the boat, killing two men.

Christopher Columbus was ill during this voyage and spent much of his time in his cabin in the Bay of Panama, where they were anchored. Despite this, he kept a close watch on the sea and weather and gave his crew instructions.

Crisis at Panama

Columbus sent Bartholomew out in one of the caravels to search the area. Panama was settled by the Ngabe people, and Bartholomew met one of their tribal chieftains, "El Quibían." El Quibían was very gracious and wore a lot of gold jewelry, which piqued Bartholomew's interest.

While exploring the coast, Bartholomew saw a great river that ran through the area. It was then the Christian feast of the Epiphany, so he called it the "Rio Belén," which stands for Bethlehem. The native names for the rivers are the Yebra and the Quiebra.

The chief firmly forbade Bartholomew to go anywhere beyond a certain point near the inland rivers, but Bartholomew ignored this and proceeded. There he found mines where, no doubt, they obtained the gold El Quibían wore.

The Spaniards built a fortress not far from the shore at the mouth of the Belén. In one part of the fortress, they kept a magazine full of ammunition. Then they built some thatched houses and tasked some of the men with creating a functional colony called "Santa María de Belén."

While the crew was finishing up work on the settlement, a crewman by the name of Diego Mendez and their interpreter were ordered to explore further. They sneaked through the forested area and came upon El Quibían's village. In the village, they noticed posts planted near the chief's hut. On top of each post was the head of a slain enemy. Diego shivered. As they eavesdropped, the interpreter heard that the villagers were plotting to attack Bartholomew and the crew near the shore. The Ngabe people clearly didn't want foreigners settling there.

Diego returned and told Bartholomew about the plot. Their interpreter then explained to Bartholomew that the natives were, most likely, angry about the construction of the little community there. Bartholomew then stationed guards by the shore and sent Diego Mendez back to Christopher Columbus to inform him.

To prevent the attack, Bartholomew had his crew go into the village heavily armed. They entered the house of the chief and bound him, along with his family and a few other warriors. Seeing the weapons the Spaniards had with them, the Ngabe put forth little resistance but offered the Spanish soldiers a "treasure" as a ransom for their king. This offer was refused. After that, Bartholomew and his men plundered the village in search of valuables they could take back to Spain.

Once back at the river, the crew tied El Quibían and the others captives to benches in their dinghy and headed back to Bartholomew and his ship. When they were a distance from the shore, the chief complained about the tightness of the rope which bound him. A compassionate member of the crew loosened it slightly. As soon as he turned his back, though, El Quibían wiggled out of the ropes, leaped into the water, and escaped. The crew pursued him, but he disappeared into the jungle. Because the river was swollen due to excessive rains, they assumed the chief had drowned.

At the ship, the strongest of the prisoners managed to escape through the hatch of the cargo hold. They attacked the crew, and some were killed. The captives then swam for shore, but several of them were re-captured and put back in the hold. In the morning, when the crew checked on the prisoners, they discovered that all of them had hung themselves with the ropes with which they were bound. Such was the depth of their fear of the Spanish.

El Quibían, whom the Spanish thought had drowned, survived and managed to work his way through the heavy jungle foliage and return to his village. Seeing the destruction and theft the Spaniards had rendered upon his people, he was furious. With vengeance in his heart, along with the acute loss of his kidnapped family, El Quibían planned to rid the area of the foreigners.

Attack at Santa María de Belén

Without warning, El Quibían and his warriors attacked the Spanish settlers at Santa María de Belén. They hurled javelins at the men and wounded many of them before retreating into the forest. Later in the day, they attacked again from their canoes, throwing darts and sending arrows through the colony. Many colonists were wounded, and some were killed. The natives kept up sporadic attacks, but the Spaniards took out their weapons and defended themselves with the strength of firepower. It worked for the time being.

The settlers knew they needed to escape, but the weather turned against them, and they were forced to hide in the fortress for protection. As the winds howled and the river waters rose, they were deeply concerned they'd run out of ammunition and food. Finally, the winds died down. They created a makeshift redoubt closer to the mouth of the river and prepared to make their escape back to the caravel.

The natives then attacked their little fortification on the shore. Diego Tristán, the captain of one of Columbus's caravels, was killed there by the natives, along with all but one other man. Bartholomew and the sailors back at the caravel were horrified when they saw their mangled corpses floating down the river.

In the Panamanian Harbor

Christopher Columbus, on his ship further out in the bay, was full of anxiety about his brother and the crew because they hadn't returned in quite some time. He prayed a great deal for their safety and wrote a long letter he intended to bring home to the king and queen. As an answer to prayer, it seemed, the seas calmed. However, there was still no sign of Bartholomew and the rest of the men. Then Christopher sent Diego Mendez and eight men into the area to look for them.

Diego located Bartholomew and the crew at their caravel—stranded on sandbanks. Shipworms, which are casually called "termites of the sea," had eaten out much of the wood on the ship, and it was no longer seaworthy. Diego then cut up some of the sails, taped two canoes together, and created a makeshift raft. With it, they rescued the harried men and traveled down the river to meet up with Christopher, who was relieved his brother was still alive but very distressed to hear of the deaths of the others at the hands of the warlike tribe.

Christopher and Bartholomew Columbus and the remaining caravels set sail for Hispaniola.

Stranded Back at Jamaica

Off the coast of Cuba, a tremendous storm erupted. Christopher and his men managed to land in Jamaica. All the ships Columbus had left were also infested with shipworms and therefore not seaworthy enough for a journey across the Atlantic. Columbus was stranded.

The Jamaicans were friendly, so Columbus was relieved he didn't have to deal with hostilities there. Columbus sent out Diego Mendez and a few men in canoes to seek help from Governor de Ovando in Hispaniola.

De Ovando was away at the time dealing with insurrections and didn't return for quite a while. When he finally returned, he delayed helping Columbus due to the grudge he nursed towards him.

Meanwhile, Columbus was running out of provisions. Luckily, he came across an astronomical chart among his things. Once he realized he could predict the next lunar eclipse, he told the Jamaican natives. He knew they were superstitious, and such a prediction would be appealing to them. Because of this, the natives provided Columbus and his crew with food.

A year after Columbus was beached in Jamaica, de Ovando sent a caravel to Jamaica, and Christopher, Diego, and Bartholomew left for Spain. They arrived in June of that year.

The End of His Journey

During the years that followed, Columbus had painful bouts of his illnesses. He was pleased with his accomplishments but finally confronted the fact that he had limitations. On his deathbed, he wrote that he had served the king and queen with loyalty and zeal but added these words: "If I have failed in anything, it has been because my knowledge and powers went no further."

He died on May 20, 1506.

Conclusion

The life of Christopher Columbus was, in a very real sense, a tragedy. As seen in these pages, Christopher Columbus struggled with the acceptance of his own frailties and errors. His life has been written in history books, but never books on human motivation. He was a man driven—not by ambition, but by purpose.

Columbus was never featured in books on advertising and sales, either, but his life stands as an example of one of the most accomplished salesmen of all time. He was a trendsetter before there were trendsetters.

He was also never featured as a man who educated himself, but he knew more than the educated men of his time. Christopher Columbus wasn't an accomplished historian, but in many ways, he rewrote history.

Here's another book by Captivating History
that you might be interested in

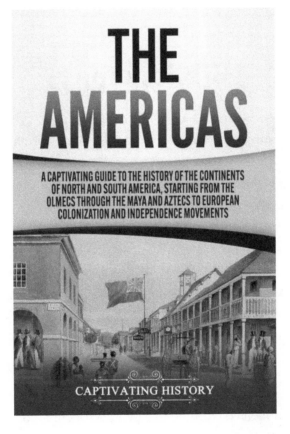

Bibliography

"Anacaona: The Haitian Queen," Retrieved from https://www.thoughtco.com/the-third-voyage-of-christopher-columbus-2136701.

"Christopher Columbus: Fourth Voyage," Retrieved from http://www.christopher-columbus.eu/voyage-4.htm#:~:text=Christopher%20Columbus%20made%20a%20fourth,from%20the%20port%20of%20Cadiz.&text=At%20age%20fifty%2Done%2C%20Columbus,more%20voyage%20left%20in%20him.

Crosby, A. W. (1987). *The Columbian Voyages, the Columbian Exchange, and Their Historians.* American Historical Assoc.

Hale, E. E. *The Life of Christopher Columbus.*

Irving, W. *The Life and Voyages of Christopher Columbus.*

"The Third Voyage of Christopher Columbus," Retrieved from https://www.thoughtco.com/the-third-voyage-of-christopher-columbus-2136701.

"The Fourth Voyage of Christopher Columbus," Retrieved from https://www.thoughtco.com/fourth-new-world-voyage-christopher-columbus-2136698#before-the-journey.

Fuson, R. H. (1992). *The Log of Christopher Columbus.* International Marine Publishing.

Keegan, W. "The Native Peoples of Turks and Caicos," Retrieved from https://www.floridamuseum.ufl.edu/caribarch/education/tc-peoples/.

"Narrative of the Third Voyage of Columbus as Contained in Las Casas' History," (2003). Wisconsin Historical Soc. Digital Library and Archives.

"Panama: Past and Present," Retrieved from https://en.wikisource.org/wiki/Panama,_past_and_present/Chapter_2.

Morison, S. E. (1942). *Admiral of the Ocean Sea*. Little, Brown & Co.

Sale, K. (1991). *The Conquest of Paradise: Christopher Columbus and the Columbian Legacy.*

"The Voyages of Christopher Columbus," Retrieved from https://www.americanjourneys.org/pdf/AJ-062.pdf.

Wey, N. (2008). *The Tropics of Empire: Why Columbus Sailed South to the Indies*. MIT Press.

Wilford, John Noble (1991). *The Mysterious History of Columbus: An Exploration of the Man, the Myth, the Legacy*. New York: Alfred A. Knopf.

Young, F. Christopher Columbus: Top Biography

"Speed under Sail of Ancient Ships," Retrieved from http://penelope.uchicago.edu/Thayer/E/Journals/TAPA/82/.

CPSIA information can be obtained
at www.ICGtesting.com
Printed in the USA
BVHW071739250122
627121BV00002B/94